W9-AJS-980

Geek out!

THE MODERN NERD'S GUIDE TO
ESPORTS

BY MATTHEW JANKOWSKI

Gareth Stevens
PUBLISHING

Please visit our website, www.garethstevens.com. For a free color catalog of all our high-quality books, call toll free 1-800-542-2595 or fax 1-877-542-2596.

Cataloging-in-Publication Data

Names: Jankowski, Matthew.
Title: The modern nerd's guide to esports / Matthew Jankowski.
Description: New York : Gareth Stevens Publishing, 2018. | Series: Geek out! | Includes index.
Identifiers: ISBN 9781538212059 (pbk.) | ISBN 9781538212073 (library bound) | ISBN 9781538212066 (6 pack)
Subjects: LCSH: Video games–Juvenile literature. | Video gamers–Juvenile literature. | Video games–Competitions.
Classification: LCC GV1469.3 J36 2018 | DDC 794.8–dc23

First Edition

Published in 2018 by
Gareth Stevens Publishing
111 East 14th Street, Suite 349
New York, NY 10003

Copyright © 2018 Gareth Stevens Publishing

Designer: Sarah Liddell
Editor: Joan Stoltman

Photo credits: Cover, p. 1 Daniel Shirey/Stringer/Getty Images Sport/Getty Images; texture used throughout StrelaStudio/Shutterstock.com; pp. 4, 7, 12, 13 Leonel Calara/Shutterstock.com; p. 5 Tinxi/Shutterstock.com; p. 9 Yann/Wikimedia Commons; pp. 10, 11 Wuestenigel/Wikimedia Commons; p. 16 Alexander Hassenstein - FIFA/Contributor/FIFA/Getty Images; p. 17 Aconcagua/Wikimedia Commons; p. 19 Czar/Wikimedia Commons; p. 20 Suzi Pratt/Contributor/FilmMagic/Getty Images; p. 21 ROBYN BECK/Staff/AFP/Getty Images; p. 25 Raynor999/Wikimedia Commons; p. 26 PhilipTerryGraham/Wikimedia Commons; p. 27 Esby/Wikimedia Commons; p. 29 Zilsonzxc/Wikimedia Commons.

All rights reserved. No part of this book may be reproduced in any form without permission in writing from the publisher, except by a reviewer.

Printed in the United States of America

CPSIA compliance information: Batch #CW18GS: For further information contact Gareth Stevens, New York, New York at 1-800-542-2595.

CONTENTS

Words in the glossary appear in **bold** type the first time they are used in the text.

A NOT-BORING HISTORY LESSON

The first sports people competed in were wrestling and running back in ancient Greece. Thousands packed into stadiums to watch **athletes** compete in the very first Olympic Games! Today, millions of people watch a new kind of sport with a new type of athlete. These **competitions** feature **aliens**, soldiers, orcs, and more!

Electronic sports, or esports, have famous players and **tournaments** from the local to the international level. Do you love gaming and competing? Esports are perfect for you! These sports rely on **strategy**, instant decision making, and quick actions. Esports are rapidly becoming as popular as sports such as football, soccer, and tennis.

As long as there have been video games, there have been video game competitions. Even one of the very first video games ever, *Pong*, let players face each other in a simple version of electronic tennis.

ESPN

The Entertainment and Sports Programming Network, or ESPN, was created in 1979. It's the leading TV network for sports news and includes eight US cable channels, 26 international channels, two radio stations, many websites, and a magazine. Recently, ESPN has started covering esports news, which can be found at *espn.com/esports*. Esports have seen huge audience growth since ESPN began reporting on them!

WHAT ARE ESPORTS?

Esports means video gaming that's been organized into competitions and is played for fans to watch. All video games are competitive, but esports are real-world competitions, not just one character against another character inside the game.

The competitions can be a tournament with friends at your home or playing other local gamers at a nearby game store. Some events are private, meaning only players that have been invited can compete. There are even huge international tournaments. Esports events can fill stadiums with thousands of fans and include gamers who are being paid to play!

THINK OF IT THIS WAY...

When you play a quick game of basketball with your friends, you're having fun while competing. The game is entertainment for you and your friends. When you join a basketball team, you play against other teams in organized competition. The game is entertainment for the crowd. Esports are the same way!

In 2016, there were 13,576 esports athletes and 3,877 esports tournaments!

LET'S GET IT STARTED!

Would you like to find yourself a home in the wonderful world of esports?

To get started, take these steps. First, pick a video game you love to play. Next, find out who the best players are and watch them play. Then read **online** guides, looking for tips, tricks, shortcuts, **glitches**, and **combos** you can use. Then play against your friends until you can beat them! Next, go online and look for local tournaments you can play in. This step is important because until you play in tournaments, you're not doing an esport. Lastly, just like any sport, you need to practice!

TOOLS OF THE TRADE

One of the most important decisions to make when trying an esport game is whether to play on a computer (PC) or a console. Neither is better, so choose whichever one you prefer! Make sure, however, that you check which esports games can be played on the console or PC you have!

Video games have come a long way since the Nintendo GameCube, but there are still tournaments for old-school games, too!

FINDING YOUR GAME

As you know, there are many different video games out there. As a future esport gamer, first take the time to find out what kind of game you like to play most. It's a good idea to download and try out free games before spending any money.

MOBAs, or multiplayer online battle arenas, are very popular in esports. In fact, the MOBA *League of Legends* (*LoL*) is currently the most popular esport—and it's free! *Dota 2* is another popular, and free, MOBA. First-person shooter (FPS) games allow players to see through the eyes of characters. *Overwatch*, one of the hottest new FPS esports, isn't free and has a league you can join.

LoL is such a popular esport that it has **professional** leagues—just like hockey, football, and other classic sports!

LEAGUE OF LEGENDS

OVERWATCH

GAME RATINGS

Overwatch isn't the only FPS esport, but it's one of the few that's rated for teenagers to play. *Counter Strike: Global Offensive* is probably the biggest FPS esport, but like the popular *Call of Duty* and *Halo* games, it's rated for ages 17 and older.

Rocket League is basically soccer with race cars you create! The game is purchased on Steam, a website for PC games and games for consoles such as XBox One and PS4. *Starcraft II* is a follow-up to one of the first esports games, *Starcraft*, from 1998. *Starcraft II* is a real-time strategy, or RTS, game, so players need to think faster than their competition. It's incredibly popular in South Korea. Maybe you can help grow its popularity here!

Hearthstone lets you collect cards and build your deck—just like you would in a collectible card game like Pokémon or Magic: The Gathering—without having to lug around hundreds of cards. Plus, it's free to play!

Street Fighter II and *Super Smash Bros.* are popular fighting games that have a lively esports fan base.

ESPORTS SPORTS?!

The esports world doesn't leave out sports video games. *Madden 18* features current National Football League (NFL) players, teams, coaches, plays, and more. *FIFA 18*, a soccer video game, allows you to play as the latest world-famous professional athletes.

TOURNAMENTS

For the fans especially, the fun in esports is all about the tournaments! Some esports have tournaments throughout the year, while others have major international events that are a lot like football's Super Bowl.

In North America, the *League of Legends* Championship Series, or LCS, runs in spring and summer. The big *Dota 2* tournament, called The International, sees teams from around the world competing to be world champion. This event also provides the chance to win the most money of any esport competition, with champions taking home over $3 million!

THE *STARCRAFT II* SCENE

Since *Starcraft II* is most popular in South Korea, the tournaments are often filled with mostly South Korean players. Gamers can win thousands of dollars at tournaments held by the Starcraft II World Championship Series put on by game-makers Blizzard Entertainment and other groups.

MOST WATCHED
ESPORTS TOURNAMENTS

TOURNAMENT	GAME	WHEN	HOW MANY PEOPLE WATCHED ONLINE
INTEL EXTREME MASTERS (IEM) KATOWICE	COUNTER STRIKE: GLOBAL OFFENSIVE (CS:GO), LEAGUE OF LEGENDS, STARCRAFT II	2017	46 MILLION
LOL WORLD CHAMPIONSHIP	LEAGUE OF LEGENDS	2016	43 MILLION
LOL WORLD CHAMPIONSHIP	LEAGUE OF LEGENDS	2015	36 MILLION
INTEL EXTREME MASTERS (IEM) KATOWICE	COUNTER STRIKE: GLOBAL OFFENSIVE (CS:GO), LEAGUE OF LEGENDS, STARCRAFT II	2016	34.1 MILLION
LOL WORLD CHAMPIONSHIP	LEAGUE OF LEGENDS	2013	32 MILLION

With these events being more and more popular, there may one day be a tournament that 1 billion people watch online!

A newly created professional *Overwatch* league has new tournaments across the country! At the Madden NFL Championship Series, gamers compete for a share of $1 million. *Rocket League* has a small, but fierce, fan base that's led to larger amounts of prize money in competitions. The Evolution Championship Series (Evo) tournament is a major worldwide event with opportunities to compete in many different esports games.

EA Sports sponsors one tournament a year called The FIFA Interactive World Cup. This event is the largest online gaming tournament in the world, with over 2.3 million players competing. The champion wins $200,000 and the chance to meet soccer stars in person!

HEARTHSTONE

Once a year, the 16 best players compete at the Hearthstone World Championship for money.

A BIG VICTORY FOR THE LITTLE GUY

Psyonix, the maker of *Rocket League*, is an independent video game maker, or developer. This means it's a small company that works without the help of big businesses. *Rocket League*'s huge following in a world where big businesses usually lead gives hope to other independent video game developers and dreamers.

THE LIFE OF THE PROS

The very best players of each esport might become professional gamers, or pros. Pros become known because they have talent for their game and know the game inside and out. They're also lucky enough to have earned chances to prove their skill in tournaments.

The life of a professional esports player isn't easy. Teams may practice for as many as 12 to 14 hours every day to keep up with the competition. Pros have to play even when they don't feel like it because there are always other hardworking gamers who want to replace them.

YES, BUT WHO'S THE BEST?

It's hard to say who's the best at *LoL* because events happen year round and it's a team game. However, many will argue that it's Faker, or Lee Sang-hyeok. He's won four world championships. His gameplay's been called "near perfect," and he's even been referred to as the Michael Jordan of *LoL*!

Once a year, teams from Europe, North America, China, South Korea, and Latin America battle in the *LoL* World Championship.

EVIL GENIUSES

THE DOTA 2 TEAM TO BEAT

The most successful *Dota 2* team is Evil Geniuses. Coming from North America, this six-person team has won 74 tournaments and over $14 million! Ukrainian team Natus Vincere, or Na'Vi, has won the most tournaments ever—92!

While some tournaments have big prizes, teams never know if they'll win. Other jobs pay you for the work you do, but esports pros usually only get paid when they win. So even when gamers are good enough to become pros, they often need other jobs outside gaming.

Some pros live-stream their practice on Twitch, where viewers can make contributions to support them. Many become sponsored, meaning that companies support them whether they win or lose as long as the pros advertise for them. Pro gamers can also make money as coaches or esports writers, or they can work at a video game company.

David "Cop" Roberson and Neil "PROLLY" Hammad are former professional *League of Legends* players who are now coaches. Cop coaches for Team Dignitas, and PROLLY coaches for H2k-Gaming.

DAVID "COP" ROBERSON

STEP ASIDE, BOYS

Unfortunately, when people think about video games, they often think they're for boys. This might make girls interested in gaming feel out of place. However, taking part in esports is a way for girls to change people's minds and show them video games aren't just a boy thing!

Even though most professional esports gamers are male, women make up 15 percent of the fans of esports, and more and more women are taking part every day. If you're a girl and enjoy gaming, you're proof that girls can be just as interested in gaming as boys!

WHO RULES THE WORLD?

Women have established themselves as gamers and in other areas of esports as well! In *League of Legends*, Eefje "Sjokz" Depoortere works as a reporter, Ryanne "Froskurinn" Mohr as a **caster**, and Kelsey Moser as a journalist and writer about all things *LoL*. Lydia Picknell has coached many professional teams in a game called *Smite*.

HIGHEST-EARNING FEMALE ESPORTS PLAYERS AND THEIR GAMES

NAME	WINNINGS TO DATE	GAME
SASHA "SCARLETT" HOSTYN	$182,805.83	STARCRAFT II
KATHERINE "MYSTIK" GUNN	$122,000.00	HALO: REACH
RICKI ORTIZ	$80,530.18	STREET FIGHTER V
MARJORIE "KASUMI CHAN" BARTELL	$55,000.00	DEAD OR ALIVE 4
SARAH "SARAH LOU" HARRISON	$50,000.00	DEAD OR ALIVE 4

These numbers are from June 2017,
but the world of esports is always changing!
Who knows who the top earner will be
in 2018, or what they'll make?

CASTERS

Love the game, but not interested in competing? You could try being a caster! Casters are the announcers or commentators of esports. If teaching others about games and describing a tournament as it plays on the battlefield sounds like something you'd like to do, you might make a great caster!

The first step is to try it out! Learn as much as possible about the ins and outs of a game and practice casting matches between friends. You could even set up a YouTube or Twitch account where you describe what's happening as you play a game, why it's happening, why that's important, and discuss information about the players.

OTHER ESPORTS JOBS

As esports grows, more and more people are able to make money working in it. Writers, **bloggers**, artists, and even **psychologists** have found a place in esports. If you love esports and have skills like writing, drawing, or understanding people, you could make your hobby a career!

LoL has a particularly active media community. Here is Sjokz, one of the North American LCS casters.

YOU CAN DO IT, TOO!

Anyone can find their place in the exciting world of esports. Whether you become a gamer, caster, writer, or fan, there's a huge community waiting to welcome you. The best way to be a part of esports is to get out and go to events, be friendly, and meet people. Some games even allow you to create your own official tournaments. *Hearthstone* lets players set up competitions known as fireside gatherings!

Once you've got your game, it's time to start competing. Any esport athlete you talk to will tell you that esports success is all about how much time you put into becoming great.

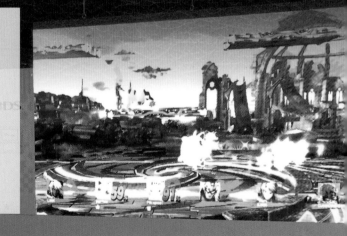

The popular *Super Smash Bros.* fighting game series has a very active community. Smash tournaments can be found on college campuses, in video-game stores, and in living rooms across the country.

THE NEED FOR SPEED

In one particular esports community, gamers are known as speed runners. These gamers attempt to finish games as fast as possible, even breaking world records! Speed runners know about the inner workings of games, using mechanics, glitches, and tricks to shorten their times. Speed runners can often be found on Twitch streaming runs.

IT'S ALL ABOUT THE FANS!

Just as with any other sport, what makes the esports world great is the fans! Luckily, it's easy to become an esports fan! Try out as many games as you can to see which ones you like most. Read about how games work and how to speak the game's language. Get inside the mind of a player and see how they make decisions during play by watching other players on YouTube or Twitch.

As a fan, offer support and energy to the world of esports. Find friends to practice with and challenge yourself against more skilled gamers. Talk about and even create new game ideas, characters, tricks, and ways to play. So much is possible in the world of esports!

WATCH AND LEARN

While many people watch sports on the ESPN or FOX Sports channels, esports fans watch matches using YouTube or Twitch. On Twitch, fans can watch professionals play live, which is called streaming. They can even watch past games and tournaments, which are called videos on demand (VODs).

Soon, there could be a huge
esports event at a stadium near you!

GLOSSARY

alien: a creature that comes from somewhere other than the planet Earth

athlete: a person who is trained in or good at sports, games, or exercises that require physical skill or strength

blogger: a person who writes personal opinions, activities, and experiences on a website

caster: someone who describes the action of a game or sports event

combo: a combination of different actions in a video game

competition: the act or process of trying to get or win something that someone else is trying to get or win

glitch: a problem in a video game that wasn't made on purpose

online: connected to a computer, or done over the internet

professional: earning money from an activity that many people do for fun

psychologist: a scientist who specializes in the study and treatment of the mind and behavior

strategy: a carefully thought-out plan, or a plan of action to achieve a goal

tournament: a sports event or series of events that involves players or teams trying to win and usually continues for several days

FOR MORE INFORMATION

BOOKS

Scholastic. *Game On! 2018: Your Guide to All the Best Games.* New York, NY: Scholastic, 2017.

Winters, Terra. *Overwatch World Guide.* New York, NY: Scholastic, 2017.

WEBSITES

Esports Kids
esportskids.com/
Read all about an esports event just for kids held in Folsom, California.

Gamepedia
gamepedia.com/
This site has an article on any video game you need to know about.

Major League Gaming
majorleaguegaming.com/
This site has links to VODs, tournament schedules, articles on esports, and player biographies.

Publisher's note to educators and parents: Our editors have carefully reviewed these websites to ensure that they are suitable for students. Many websites change frequently, however, and we cannot guarantee that a site's future contents will continue to meet our high standards of quality and educational value. Be advised that students should be closely supervised whenever they access the Internet.

INDEX